Ownership and Asymmetric Information Problems in the Corporate Loan Market: Evidence from a Heteroskedastic Regression

Lewis Gaul and Viktors Stebunovs

Economics and Policy Analysis Working Paper 2009-1

April 2009

Ownership and Asymmetric Information Problems in the Corporate Loan Market: Evidence from a Heteroskedastic Regression

Lewis Gaul and Viktors Stebunovs

April 2009

OCC Economics Working Paper 2009-1

1. Introduction

In credit markets, asymmetric information problems arise when borrowers have private information about their creditworthiness that is not observable by lenders. If these informational asymmetries do not negatively affect lenders' profitability, then they are irrelevant to lenders (Chiappori and Salanie (2000), Chiappori et al. (2006)). However, a large literature articulates conditions under which asymmetric information is relevant to lenders as a consequence of adverse selection and moral hazard problems (Jaffee and Russell (1976), Stiglitz and Weiss (1981)).[1] While numerous articles document the theoretical importance of asymmetric information problems in credit markets, few empirical studies provide direct empirical evidence regarding either the existence of asymmetric information problems or lenders' efforts to overcome them (Ausubel (1999), Ivashina (2008), Sufi (2007)).

In this paper, we provide empirical evidence that asymmetric information problems exist in the corporate loan market, and that loan ownership provides incentives for lenders to allocate resources to overcoming these problems. Our investigation is based on the assertion of Leland and Pyle (1977) that ownership provides lenders with the incentive to overcome adverse selection problems by screening borrowers to elicit their private information.[2] Using a heteroskedastic regression, we provide evidence that there is a statistically significant positive association between publicly unobservable information imputed into corporate loan interest rate spreads, and ownership of loans by lenders with responsibility for negotiating loan contract terms. However, the amount of unobservable information imputed into loan interest rate spreads is similar for loans provided by a single lender and syndicated loans similar in ownership structure to loans provided by a single lender.[3] Our results are consistent with the following assertions: (1) adverse selection and/or moral hazard problems exist in the corporate loan market; (2) ownership stakes provide lenders with the necessary incentives to acquire borrowers' private information; and (3) originating loans for distribution weakens, but does not eliminate, lenders' incentives to solve asymmetric information problems. We identify adverse selection and/or moral hazard problems through the association between unobservable information incorporated into loan spreads and loan ownership, as predicted by the theory of Leland and Pyle (1977).[4]

---

[1]For the remainder of the text, we will occasionally refer to the combination of adverse selection and/or moral hazard problems more succinctly as asymmetric information problems.

[2]While Leland and Pyle (1977) describe adverse selection problems, the implications of their model are generalizable to both adverse selection and moral hazard problems. For instance, Holmstrom and Tirole (1997) present a theoretical model where ownership provides lenders with the incentive to monitor borrowers' ex-post to overcome moral hazard problems.

[3]Syndicated loans with ownership structures similar to loans provided by a single lender are syndicated loans with fewer lenders and syndicated loans where lead lenders retain large ownership stakes.

[4]We interpret unobservable information imputed into loan spreads as evidence of ex-ante screening. This is based upon

This paper makes several contributions. Our main contribution is providing evidence regarding the existence of asymmetric information problems in credit markets and lenders' efforts to overcome these problems.[5] Few studies provide direct evidence of asymmetric information problems in credit markets. Ausubel (1999) provides evidence that adverse selection exists in the credit card market. He presents evidence that unobservable information that induces credit card customers to choose less favorable credit card terms is associated with a greater likelihood of default. Sufi (2007) presents evidence lead lenders in loan syndicates retain smaller ownership shares in loans after building a relationship with borrowers, which is consistent with existence of moral hazard, and relationships overcoming moral hazard problems.[6] Ivashina (2008) provides evidence that greater ownership stakes retained by lead lenders mitigates asymmetric information problems between lead lenders and participant lenders in loan syndicates.

This paper contributes to the literature that examines the empirical determinants of loan syndication. Our results provide additional evidence that ownership of loans by lead banks in loan syndicates may be used to provide lenders incentives to solve asymmetric information problems. Previous research documents a positive association between variables that are likely to indicate asymmetric information problems, such as the availability of public financial statements or research and development expenditures, and lead lenders' retained ownership shares in syndicated loans (Dennis and Mullineaux (2000), Jones et al. (2000), Preece and Mullineaux (1996)). These studies suggest that lead lender ownership is used to provide incentives for lenders to solve asymmetric information problems; however, these results do not directly indicate that publicly unobservable information, relevant to lenders' profitability, exists. Our results suggest the presence of asymmetric information problems in the corporate loan market by providing evidence that lead lenders incorporate more unobservable information into loan spreads when they retain larger ownership stakes in syndicated loans.

Our paper also contributes to the policy debate regarding whether the originate-to-distribute model

---

the assumption that lenders would charge borrowers interest rates based on observable risk characteristics in the absence of asymmetric information problems, and the expected value of borrowers' private information.

[5]This paper also contributes to the wider literature regarding the existence of asymmetric information. Several studies have examined evidence of asymmetric information in other markets such as the insurance and annuity markets.

[6]A syndicated loan is a loan with two or more lenders. Typically, a lead lender negotiates the terms of a loan contract directly with a borrower for an agreed-upon range of interest rates. The lead lender then uses the negotiated terms of the loan contract to solicit participant lenders to provide a portion of the loans' funding. Usually, lead lenders provide funding for the residual portion of the loan that remains after soliciting financing from participants; lead lenders typically transfer as much ownership of loans to participants as possible. Lead lenders are responsible for mitigating potential asymmetric information problems.

of bank lending is detrimental to the safety and soundness of the banking system.[7] In a recent speech, Comptroller of the Currency John C. Dugan raised concerns that lenders now underwrite loans with the incentive to increase the likelihood that loans will be sold rather than repaid.[8] Our results are consistent with these concerns, as they suggest that lenders expend less effort solving asymmetric information problems, ex-ante, when they retain smaller ownership stakes in loans. Hence, lenders negotiating loan contract terms are not taking steps, ex-ante, to mitigate the impact that adverse selection and/or moral hazard problems may potentially have on a loan's profitability. Our results suggest that further research is warranted regarding how the originate-to-distribute model of lending influences lenders incentives to solve asymmetric information problems.

2. Related Literature

The seminal contributions of Akerlof (1970) and Rothchild and Stiglitz (1976) articulate that asymmetric information is relevant in competitive markets when the private, publicly unobservable information possessed by one party to a transaction is relevant to another party's profitability. Jaffee and Russell (1976) and Stiglitz and Weiss (1981) provide theoretical models with the implication that adverse selection and/or moral hazard can lead to credit rationing in a competitive market. In their models, borrowers know their creditworthiness, while lenders do not; any attempt by lenders to differentiate (screen) borrowers by raising interest rates leads to a reduction in their profitability, as more creditworthy borrowers drop out of the market when interest rates rise beyond a certain threshold.

Leland and Pyle (1977) first suggested loan ownership stakes provide incentives for lenders to overcome asymmetric information problems. They present a model where entrepreneurs have an investment opportunity, but have insufficient to funds to finance the project. In addition, entrepreneurs know their own creditworthiness, which is unobservable to lenders. Entrepreneurs can signal their creditworthiness to lenders by retaining large equity stakes in the project. Since entrepreneurs are risk adverse, they prefer to sell ownership of the project to third parties and invest the proceeds in a diversified portfolio of assets; hence, ownership stakes expose entrepreneurs to non-diversifiable idiosyncratic risk, providing lenders with a credible signal that the borrowers are creditworthy. At the end of the paper, Leland and Pyle speculate

---

[7]Originating a loan for distribution implies that lenders negotiate loan contract terms with the intention of transferring all or part of a loan to a third-party lender. A syndicated loan is one type of loan that is originated for distribution.

[8]Speech before the American Bankers Association on October 8, 2007.

4

how entrepreneurs' retained ownership stakes relate to ownership of loans by lenders, such as banks. They speculate that lenders could issue deposits and invest in large ownership stakes in loans, exposing lenders to idiosyncratic risk, which provides lenders with a credible incentive to ascertain borrowers' private information regarding their own creditworthiness. Diamond (1984) presents a theoretical model formalizing this intuition. Holmstrom and Tirole (1997) present a similar model where lenders retain ownership stakes in loans to credibly commit to overcoming moral hazard problems.

Recently, the proliferation of the syndicated loan market has motivated empirical research testing the intuition of Leland and Pyle (1977) and Holmstrom and Tirole (1997) that ownership of loans provides lenders with incentives to overcome asymmetric information problems. In a syndicated loan contract a borrower receives a loan from two or more lenders. Typically, a lead lender negotiates the terms of the loan contract with a borrower for an agreed-upon range of interest rates, and subsequently uses the negotiated loan contract terms to solicit a group of participant lenders. In these agreements, the lead lender bears responsibility for screening borrowers' creditworthiness. In a syndicated lending arrangement, two types of asymmetric information potentially exist: (1) borrowers may have private information regarding their creditworthiness that is unobservable to lenders, and (2) lead lenders may acquire private information regarding the borrowers' credit worthiness that is unobservable to participant lenders. Standard adverse selection and/or moral hazard problems arise from both types of asymmetric information problems, and ownership by lenders is predicted to overcome problems arising from both types of asymmetric information problems.[9]

Recent research by Sufi (2007) provides evidence consistent with the prediction of Holmstrom and Tirole (1997) that ownership shares provide lead lenders with the incentive to overcome asymmetric information problems, in particular moral hazard problems. He provides evidence of a positive association between the share of the loan retained by lead lenders and several proxies for adverse selection and/or moral hazard problems; in addition, he provides direct evidence of moral hazard problems, with the result that lead lenders retain smaller ownership stakes in loans after developing a lending relationship with borrowers. Ivashina (2008) provides empirical evidence regarding the implications of asymmetric information problems between lead lenders and participant lenders. She asserts that these asymmetric information problems between lead lenders and participant lenders result in borrowers paying greater interest rate spreads on syndicated loans.

---

[9]The former informational asymmetry leads to the standard adverse selection and moral hazard problem described by Jaffee and Russell (1976) and Stiglitz and Weiss (1981); the informational asymmetry leads to adverse selection problems as lead lenders wish to syndicate their riskiest loans and moral hazard problems, because a reduction in ownership reduces incentives to monitor borrowers ex-post.

She tests Leland and Pyle's prediction that greater ownership stakes retained by lead lenders alleviate this asymmetric information problem. She finds that lead lenders' ownership shares are negatively associated with interest rate spreads on syndicated loans, confirming Leland and Pyle's predictions.

3. Empirical exercise

Our objective is to examine whether, holding all else constant, there exists a positive and statistically significant association between the amount of publicly unobservable information incorporated into corporate loan spreads and ownership of loans by lead lenders in loan syndicates. We conjecture that the variation in loan interest rate spreads unexplained by publicly observable information adequately captures borrowers' private information about their own creditworthiness, gathered by lenders during their ex-ante assessment of borrowers' creditworthiness.[10] We examine the relationship between ownership and unobservable information incorporated into loan spreads in order to provide evidence that asymmetric information problems exist in the corporate loan market, and that ownership provides lenders with the incentive to overcome asymmetric information problems. It is important to note that failure to find evidence of a statistically significant association between ownership and loan spread dispersion does not imply that asymmetric information problems do not exist. Our approach must identify asymmetric information problems and ownership mitigating asymmetric information problems simultaneously. We hypothesize that if asymmetric information problems do exist, there will be a positive association between unobservable information incorporated into loan spreads and ownership, as predicted by Leland and Pyle (1977).

However, we note several complications in attempting to achieve this objective. For example, several studies show that lenders incorporate information regarding their own financial state into loan contract terms. Sufi (2007) and Ivashina (2008) suggest that banks may attempt to price the idiosyncratic risk or total exposure faced in lending to a borrower into loan interest rate spreads. Hubbard et al. (2002) provide evidence that banks with low levels of equity capital to assets charge greater interest rate spreads. Hence, we also attempt control for the financial state of lenders with responsibility for negotiating loan contract

---

[10]We assume that lenders would not have incentives to gather unobservable information unless adverse selection and/or moral hazard problems exist, because even if lenders charge borrowers different interest rates according to their true creditworthiness (based on observable and unobservable private information), the lender would earn the same average rate of return that would be earned by charging observably identical borrowers an interest rate based on the expected value of borrowers' private information, without paying a cost to acquire the private information. We argue that our approach is reasonable if there are costs to acquiring borrowers' private unobservable information.

terms. We admit that it is difficult to adequately control for lenders' financial state. In addition, discouragingly, we speculate that lenders should impute more information regarding their own financial state into loan contract terms when they retain larger ownership stakes. Consequently, if we are unable to adequately account for lenders' financial state, we expect that this would make it easier to find a positive association between unobserved information imputed into loan spreads and lenders' ownership stakes.

In addition, another complication when examining the association between ownership and unobservable information imputed into loan spreads is that ownership of loans may merely proxy for borrowers' asymmetric information problems. Hence, it is important to control for other loan contract terms that may indicate the existence of asymmetric information problems. Several studies provide empirical evidence that lenders with responsibility for monitoring borrowers are forced to retain larger ownership stakes when asymmetric information problems are potentially more severe. Hence, ownership may merely capture borrowers' asymmetric information problems, rather than the incentive to overcome asymmetric information problems provided by ownership. Therefore, we attempt to exhaustively control for observable proxies that could indicate the existence of asymmetric information problems, where our proxies are derived from previous research.[11] Consequently, we include information regarding other loan contract terms which may proxy for asymmetric information problems and better explain lenders' incentive to overcome these problems.

In our empirical exercise we use the heteroskedastic regression proposed by Harvey (1976). The heteroskedastic regression can be summarized as an empirical model containing two equations: (1) a regression equation explaining the mean of a dependent variable, and (2) an equation explaining the variance of the residuals in the regression equation.[12] In our exercise, the first equation, the regression equation, explains the mean of corporate loan interest rate spreads with a set of publicly available information; the second equation explains the variance of the residuals of the first equation, which we interpret as the variance of unobserved information imputed into loan interest rates.

Two recent empirical papers have used the same methodology for similar examinations. Degryse et al. (2007) examine the determinants of unexplained variation (the variance of the residuals of a regression describing loan interest rates) in interest rate spreads in loans to small businesses, and attribute the unex-

---

[11]Studies suggesting empirical proxies for borrowers' asymmetric information problems include but are not limited to Carey et al. (1998), Dennis and Mullineaux (2000), Ivashina (2008), Jones et al. (2000), Lee and Mullineaux (2004), Strahan (1999), and Sufi (2007).

[12]For a full discussion of the heteroskedastic regression, see Cerqueiro, Degryse, and Ongena (2008).

plained variation to banks' "discretionary use of market power in the loan rate setting process." In addition, Iannotta (2008) examines unexplained variation in the interest rate spreads for subordinated bond issues by European banks, and interprets unexplained variation in bond spreads as unobservable information imputed into loan terms by bond investors, where the unobserved information is gathered through bond investors' ex-ante screening of banks' credit quality. Our approach is most similar to that of Iannotta (2008), as we attribute unexplained variation as unobservable information regarding borrowers' creditworthiness imputed into loan interest rate spreads gathered during lenders' initial ex-ante credit screening. A primary difference with prior research is that we are attempting to examine variation in spreads after controlling only for publicly available information regarding borrowers' risk characteristics. Prior research has included numerous other control variables in the mean equation, such as those describing other loan contract terms. However, we omit such variables, as information regarding other loan contract terms could contain borrowers' private information that has been gathered during lenders' ex-ante credit evaluation.

Our heteroskedastic regression model is provided by the following empirical model:

$$Y_{i,t} = \beta'X + \epsilon_{i,t} \tag{1}$$

$$\sigma_{i,t}^2 = e^{\gamma'Z} \tag{2}$$

In our heteroskedastic regression model, our regression model is describing the mean, $Y_{i,t}$, provided by equation (1), and the model describing the residual variance, $\sigma_{i,t}^2$, is provided by equation (2). The subscripts in equations (1) and (2) refer to borrower, i, during year, t. The dependent variable in equation (1) is the interest rate spread. The interest rate spread is explained by a matrix of independent explanatory variables X, which we will describe shortly, which is multiplied by parameter vector β; the term $\epsilon_{i,t}$ is the white-noise error, which we interpret as the unobserved private information gathered by the bank in their ex-ante credit evaluation. In equation (2), the residual variance of the error term is explained by a matrix of explanatory variables Z, with vector of coefficients, γ.

We utilize several control variables in the X and Z matrices. As previously mentioned, the core set of

8

explanatory variables is intended to proxy for borrowers' observable risk characteristics and the likelihood of borrowers' asymmetric information problems, which we draw from the previous literature examining the empirical determinants of corporate loan contract terms.[13] In addition, we include proxies for lenders' financial state, which is intended to proxy for information regarding lenders' financial state that may be priced into syndicated loan contract terms or influence lenders' incentives to solve asymmetric information problems. The observable risk characteristics are derived from borrowers' financial statement data obtained from COMPUSTAT, borrowers' stock market data from CRSP, and debt ratings from COMPUSTAT. Proxies describing lenders' financial states are gathered from bank holding company financial data included from the Federal Reserve Y-9C (FR Y-9C) call report forms.[14,15] The Z matrix contains all control variables included in the X matrix, in addition to the other control variables intended to capture loan ownership by lenders with responsibility for negotiating loan contract terms, and other loan contract terms. We must exhaustively control for other variables that potentially indicate asymmetric information problems, because our intention is for our ownership variables to capture lenders' incentives to gather borrowers' private information, rather than the mere existence of asymmetric information problems.[16] All variables capturing borrowers' observable risk characteristics and the likelihood of borrowers' having asymmetric information problems are observed from the fiscal year prior to the loan contract, in order to ensure that this information proxies for the set that would have been used by lenders when negotiating loan contract terms. In addition, all lender control variables are also observed from the fiscal year prior to the loan contract. In addition, all other loan contract terms used as control variables in equation (1) are obviously observed at the same date as the loan interest rate spread.

---

[13]This literature includes, but is not limited to; Carey et al. (1998); Hubbard et al. (2002); Qian and Strahan (2007); and Strahan (1999).

[14]We only include data on lenders that are part of large bank holding companies due to data limitations. An issue arises in deciding whether to focus on individual bank data or holding company report data. We focus on the holding company level because syndicated loans in our data sample are very large loans on average. Hence, we argue that it is likely that the terms of these loan contracts are likely to be influenced by the financial state of the entire holding company rather than an individual bank in a holding company. In addition, holding company data allow us to include loans made by non-bank subsidiaries of bank holding companies.

[15]We include holding company data for lead lenders in syndicated loans as these banks are likely those responsible for negotiating syndicated loan contract terms. We follow the approach of Ivashina (2008) in determining lead lenders. Our data on lead lenders' identities and ownership shares is derived from the "Lenders-All Lenders" data item in the DEALSCAN. Because there is no known link between the DEALSCAN database and the FR Y-9C data, we match lead lenders identified by the DEALSCAN database to lenders' financial statement data from FR Y-9C by name. We include only unambiguous matches between lead lenders and associated holding companies.

[16]For example, lenders may solve asymmetric information problems through ex-ante screening regardless of loan ownership, or may elicit borrowers' private information with other loan contract features, and may just happen to be forced to retain larger stakes in loans when asymmetric information problems are likely to be severe. Hence, other observable proxies for asymmetric information problems or loan contract terms may explain away any positive association between ownership and unobservable information imputed into loan contract terms.

We construct multiple measures of loan ownership. Our first measure is a dummy variable indicating whether or not a loan is syndicated. This variable is intended to capture whether or not there is a difference in lenders' incentive to gather non-public information between loans whose lenders retain full ownership (sole lender loans) and loans where lenders retain less than full ownership (syndicated loans). Our second measures are based on the number of lenders. Sole lenders have a single lender, while syndicated loans have multiple lenders. This measure is available after 1999 in our data set. This variable does not capture lenders' ownership share; however, it is likely that lead lenders in syndicate loans retain smaller ownership stakes when there are multiple lenders. The number of lenders is a noisy proxy for ownership, which should make it more difficult to find evidence consistent with a priori expectations. We include the number of lenders as the log of 1 plus the number of lenders. Another measure of ownership is lenders' retained ownership share in the loan.[17] Lenders' ownership share is included as the log of the percent of the loan owned by the sole or lead lender in the syndicate. We also allow estimate specifications intended to examine whether the association between unobservable information in loan spreads and ownership is nonlinear. So we construct indicators for quartiles of the number of lenders and loan ownership shares.

The overlapping variables in the X and Z matricies can be grouped into three categories: those describing borrowers' credit risk, those describing borrowers' asymmetric information problems, and variables describing lenders' financial state. In equation (1) variables indicating greater credit risk or asymmetric information problems should be associated with greater borrowing costs. Greater credit risk increases borrowing costs as lenders expect the likelihood of default to increase, which lowers the expected return to lending to a borrower. Greater asymmetric information problems cause lenders to exert greater effort monitoring borrowers, which increases borrowing costs as lenders demand compensation for monitoring efforts. Asymmetric information problems imply that lenders must exert greater effort ex-ante to distinguish borrowers' creditworthiness (adverse selection and/or moral hazard) and/or greater effort examining whether borrowers are taking risks ex-post that are not in the lenders' interests (moral hazard). In equation (2), greater monitoring effort exerted by banks should be associated with greater unexplained variation in loan interest rate spreads, captured by an increase in the variance of the residuals $\sigma_{i,t}^2$.

We include several proxies that capture the likelihood of a borrower having asymmetric information problems. We include a proxy for how many times a borrower has accessed the corporate loan market,

---

[17] We include loans where there exists only a single lead lender.

10

as captured by the number of previous deals exisiting for a borrower in the DEALSCAN database. This variable is intended to capture any decline in asymmetric information from repeated interactions between borrowers and the corporate loan market.[18] We include a proxy for firms' size, as larger firms are likely to have survived a long time and have more information produced about their financial state, which may reduce the need for banks to produce information ex-ante. For example, even if unobservable information exists regarding larger borrowers' creditworthiness, the information may have been learned over time by financial market participants such as the lenders, or transmitted by other sources such as security analysts. Hence, we predict that larger firms are less likely to suffer from asymmetric information problems. However, we may expect more unobservable information to be imputed into loan spreads for larger firms if information we do not observe has been produced and disseminated by other sources and subsequently observed by banks; however, we speculate that stock market valuations and debt ratings may adequately capture any of this information. We calculate borrower size and the log of total assets (COMPUSTAT item6).

We include two proxies for borrowers' growth options. We include research and development expense, which is calculated as research and development expense divided by total assets (item46/item6).[19] Firms with greater levels of research and development spending are typically thought to have greater growth opportunities, which creates both ex-ante and ex-post asymmetric information problems. It is difficult to ascertain these borrowers' creditworthiness ex-ante (adverse selection), and prohibit their owners from shifting risks ex-post in a manner inconsistent with lenders' interests (moral hazard). In addition, we include another proxy for borrowers' growth opportunities, the market-to-book ratio, which is calculated as the sum of the market value of firms' equity plus the book value of debt divided by total assets ((stock price*shares outstanding from CRSP + item34 + item9)/item6). While greater growth opportunities, as indicated by the market-to-book ratio, are expected to be associated with greater asymmetric information problems, the market-to-book ratio also indicates greater expected profitability, which may indicate less credit risk. Hence, we do not have any strong prediction regarding the association between the market-to-book ratio and loan spreads, but expect the market-to-book ratio to be associated with greater asymmetric information problems.

We include the standard deviation of stock returns and stock trading volume as proxies for asymmetric information problems. Firms with volatile stock returns and greater stock trading volume frequently have

---

[18]We also include a measure of the number of previous deals between a borrower and the sole lender or lead lender. However, results were not significant, and were omitted to relieve estimation difficulties.

[19]We code missing values as zero and create a dummy variable equal to 1 when the data item is not missing.

had new information imputed into their stock market valuations. Therefore, we expect that it may be more difficult for lenders to acquire or understand larger quantities of new information that has been imputed into borrowers' valuations, which may be associated with an increase in asymmetric information. In addition, more volatile stock returns may indicate greater uncertainty, which could increase asymmetric information problems and credit risk. The standard deviation of stock returns is calculated as the standard deviation of daily stock returns for the entire fiscal year, where stock returns are calculated as borrowers' daily return excluding dividends from CRSP minus the CRSP value-weighted index daily return, excluding dividends.

We now describe several proxies for borrowers' credit risk. We include a proxy for a borrowers' debt rating, which is the Standard and Poor's Long Term Domestic Issuer credit rating from COMPUSTAT item280. The COMPUSTAT manual states that this variable indicates borrowers' capacity and willingness to repay debt. COMPUSTAT presents the debt rating variable as a numeric value for each rating (i.e., AAA, AA+). We recode the debt rating as a value of 1 for the most favorable debt rating of AAA, and impose increasing values as debt ratings decline until the least favorable debt rating of D.[20] We include a proxy for firms' leverage ratio, which is calculated as the sum of borrowers' short-term and long-term debt divided by total assets ((item34+item9)/item6). Firms with greater leverage ratios, holding all else constant, are more likely to default on debt obligations, and are expected to have greater credit risk. We include a proxy for borrowers' ability to generate revenues to meet interest payments on debt, calculated as borrowers' total interest expense divided by total sales (item15/item12). Firms with a greater amount of revenues pledged to interest payments are more likely to have difficulties repaying debts, which should be associated with greater credit risk. We include the quick ratio, which captures the quantity of short-term assets available to cover short-term liabilities, which is calculated as current assets less inventories, all divided by current liabilities ((item4-item3)/item5). Firms with more short-term (near cash) assets relative to short-term liabilities are more likely to make short-term debt payments and have less short-term credit risk. Our final credit risk proxy is the portion of total debt due in one year, which is calculated as debt due in one year divided by the sum of long-term and short-term debt (item44/(item34+item9)). If a borrower has a greater amount of debt due on a short time horizon, then we expect a borrower to have greater short-term credit risk.

We also include data on non-price loan contract terms in the equation for the variance of the residuals. Several non-price loan contract terms may be utilized by lenders to mitigate problems associated with credit

---

[20]We code missing values as zero and create a dummy variable for missing debt ratings.

risk or asymmetric information problems. The non-price loan terms intended to deal with asymmetric information problems may elicit borrowers' private information independent of ex-ante screening, or indicate the existence of asymmetric information problems solved with greater ex-ante monitoring independent of ownership. All data for the non-price loan contract terms comes from the DEALSCAN database. We include the size of the loans' facility amount, which is the log of the facility amount in dollars. Larger loans present greater credit risk to lenders, which should be associated with greater credit risk. However, larger borrowers suffering less from asymmetric information problems are also more likely to receive larger loans, and if our proxies for borrowers' asymmetric information problems are inadequate, then we might expect loan amount to be associated with greater dispersion in the residuals.[21] We include the maturity length of a loan, which we measure as the log of loans' maturity length in days. Theoretical models provide conflicting predictions regarding the link between the maturity length of a debt contract and borrowers' credit risk and/or asymmetric information problems. Diamond (1991) presents a model where the most creditworthy and least creditworthy firms borrow at short maturities, and borrowers with average creditworthiness borrow at long maturities. Flannery (1986) presents a model where borrowers with the highest level of creditworthiness borrow at the shortest maturity. Since our DEALSCAN database tends to include the largest, most creditworthy borrowers, we expect that maturity length may be inversely related to borrowers' credit quality and/or asymmetric information problems. We include a dummy variable indicating whether a loan is secured. Booth and Booth (2006) present evidence that less creditworthy borrowers and borrowers with greater asymmetric information problems pledge collateral, and that loan spreads on secured loans are lower after controlling for the endogeneity of loans' secured status. In addition, Strahan (1999) presents evidence that secured, syndicated loans carry greater interest-rate spreads than unsecured, syndicated loans.[22] Since we are unable to control for the endogeneity of a loan being secured in equilibrium as in Booth and Booth, we expect secured loans to be associated with greater asymmetric information problems. We include dummy variables for whether loans have covenants. Covenants are typically utilized to monitor borrowers' ex-post actions, which mitigates moral hazard problems. Therefore, we expect covenants to capture greater asymmetric information problems. Our final control variable for non-price loan terms includes a dummy variable indicating whether a loan contract contains performance pricing. Performance pricing is a contract stipulation that the interest rate spread will adjust according to changes in borrowers' financial statement performance, such as an increase or decrease in EBITDA. Performance pricing, if included in a loan contract,

---

[21]Strahan (1999) presents evidence that more observably creditworthy firms receive larger loans, and that larger loans carry lower spreads over LIBOR.

[22]When the secured variable is missing in the data, we code these values as 0; we include a dummy variable equal to 1 when the secured variable is not missing.

may solve either adverse selection and/or moral hazard problems and likely substitutes for ex-ante and/or ex-post screening.

Our final control variables attempt to adequately control for the lenders' financial state. We include proxies for lenders' size, equity capital, and amount of loan loss provisions. Our proxy for lenders' size is the log of total assets. Larger lenders likely have lasted a long while and built a favorable reputation with financial markets and likely have a low cost of capital and can lend at lower interest rate spreads. Larger lenders also likely have sophisticated information technology systems and superior resources to gather information about borrowers' credit worthiness, which may induce lenders to engage in greater amounts of ex-ante screening. Our proxy for equity capital is total equity capital divided by total assets. We include equity capital because lenders with more equity may be less likely to become insolvent and be better able to sustain loan losses. This, in turn, may lower their cost of capital allowing the lender to charge lower interest rates on loans. Hubbard et al. (2002) provide empirical evidence that syndicated loan spreads reported in DEALSCAN are greater for lead lenders with low capital ratios. In addition, if lenders with more equity capital are less likely to become insolvent, they have less incentive to engage in ex-ante screening to mitigate asymmetric information problems. Our proxy for loan loss provisions is calculated as total loan loss provisions divided by total assets. Loan loss provisions are used by lenders as a reserve for expected future loan losses; hence, lenders with greater loan loss provisions may be more likely to become insolvent and have a greater cost of capital as a result. Therefore, lenders with greater loan loss provisions may charge higher interest rates on syndicated loans. In addition, lenders with more loan provisions may have greater incentive to engage in greater ex-ante screening of borrowers in order to improve the performance of future loans and avoid worsening financial condition.

4. Summary Statistics

The summary statistics are presented in Table (1). The statistics indicate that the average firm in our sample is large and of high credit quality. In addition, the firms in our data sample are larger and appear to be of a relatively high credit quality compared to firms included in prior research. For instance, the average size of firms in our data sample is roughly 4.3 billion dollars in assets, and the firm pays an average interest rate spread over LIBOR of 153 basis points. This contrasts with previous research by Strahan (1999) where borrowers on average have about 2.4 billion dollars in assets, and pay an average spread of about 185 basis points. Sufi (2007), who also examines asymmetric information in the syndicated loan market using

DEALSCAN and COMPUSTAT data, has borrowers with an average of about 3.3 billion dollars in total assets, paying an average spread of 159 basis points. In addition, compared to Sufi (2007), our borrowers on average have higher EBITDA and lower leverage. Therefore, it appears our borrowers qualitatively may have fewer asymmetric information problems and be of greater creditworthiness than those included in previous research. Any potential bias should make it more difficult to find evidence that asymmetric information problems exist in the corporate loan market.

The statistics are grouped into five main categories: (1) asymmetric information controls, (2) credit risk controls, (3) non-price loan terms, (4) ownership controls and loan spreads, and (5) lead lender characteristics. We briefly describe our main control variables. The standard deviation of interest rate spreads is roughly 114 basis points with a mean of about 153 basis points, which indicates that there is substantial variation in interest rate spreads. In addition, the average loan has roughly nine lenders with a standard deviation of 9, and lead lenders retain roughly 38 percent ownership of a loan with a standard deviation of about 36 percent. These statistics indicate that there is significant variation in loan ownership to exploit in our empirical estimations.

5. Estimation Results

Our main results are presented in Tables (2)-(7). The estimation results for equation (1) are presented in Tables (2), (4), and (6); the results for equation (2) are presented in Tables (3), (5), and (6). We briefly describe the results for equation (1), and then focus thoroughly on the results for the residual variance equation. The parameter estimates across specifications appear to be qualitatively consistent, which is encouraging given that different specifications include different sample periods and sample sizes. In addition, the parameter estimates appear to be generally consistent with the empirical prediction that variables that proxy for greater credit risk or asymmetric information should be associated with greater loan spreads.

The first rows contain the variables that are intended to primarily capture credit risk. The parameter estimates for leverage and EBITDA are statistically significant at the 1 percent level in nearly all columns, with exception of the results in Table (6). The coefficient on leverage is positive in all columns, which is consistent with the empirical predictions that increased default risk is associated greater loan spreads. The coefficient on EBITDA is negative, as predicted, consistent with greater profitability resulting in lower loan

15

spreads. Parameter estimates for variables capturing borrowers' short-term credit risk, which include debt due in one year, the quick ratio, and the current ratio, are generally consistent with empirical predictions; however, the parameter estimates are not always statistically different from zero and the level of statistical significance of parameter estimates varies across specifications. Statistical significance is not a primary concern in equation (1), as we are attempting to exhaustively capture the set of publicly available information banks may use. Including numerous controls may cause multicollinearity, inflating the standard errors of the coefficient estimates. The only result inconsistent with our predictions is that the coefficient on the quick ratio, which we predict to be associated with less short-term credit risk, is positive. The coefficient on our final proxy for credit risk, dividends, is positive but not statistically different from zero in Tables (2) and (4), and the coefficients are negative and sometimes statistically significant in Table (6).

We next describe the results for variables we expect to be primarily associated with asymmetric information problems. As predicted, stock return volatility and research and development expense have positive associations with loan spreads in all models. The parameter estimates for stock return volatility are statistically different from zero at the 1 percent level in all specifications, while some coefficients for research and development are statistically significant in Tables (2) and (4). We provided no strict empirical predictions of how the market-to-book ratio or stock trading volume captures asymmetric information problems faced by borrowers. The coefficient on the market-to-book ratio is negative and only sometimes statistically significant in Table (6). The coefficients on trading volume are negative in all specifications, and statistically significant at varying levels in Tables (2) and (4).

The remaining estimates are for coefficients on the variables describing lead lenders' financial state. Lead bank capital ratios have a negative association with loan spreads, as expected, but the coefficients are not statistically different from zero. As predicted, loan loss provisions have a positive association with loan spreads, but only a few of the coefficients are statistically significant in Table (4). Bank assets, as predicted, have a negative association with loan spreads, and coefficient estimates are statistically different from zero at the 1 percent level in all estimations.

Tables (3), (5), and (7) present results for numerous specifications of equation (2), where specifications vary with measures of lead lender ownership, and, within each measure of loan ownership, specifications are presented with and without non-price loan contract terms. Table (3) presents specifications where loan ownership is captured with the dummy variable indicating whether or not a loan is syndicated. This specification is intended to capture whether there is a statistically significant difference in lead ex-ante information production between sole lender and syndicated loans. The results in the first column indicate a negative association between a loan being syndicated and the residual variance of the loan spread model, which is statistically significant at the 5 percent level. However, upon including non-price loan terms in column (2), the coefficient on the syndicated loan dummy is negative but no longer statistically significant. These results imply that there is no statistically significant difference in lead lenders' ex-ante monitoring efforts for syndicated and sole lender loans, and that any difference in residual variance between sole lender and syndicated loans is captured by non-price loan terms. These results are consistent with the assertion that syndication alone has not been associated with a reduction in lenders' efforts to solve asymmetric information problems.

Table (5) presents results of specifications where loan ownership is captured by the number of lenders. In columns (1)-(4), all results include both sole lender and syndicated loans, and results in columns (5)-(8) pertain only to syndicated loans. In the first two columns, the coefficient on the log of the number of lenders is negative and statistically significant at the 1 percent level; however, the coefficient is smaller after including non-price loan terms. These parameter estimates imply that doubling the number of lenders decreases the residual variance by 9 percent. The results in columns (3) and (4) include dummy variables for quartiles of lenders in syndicated loans; no dummy variable is included for sole lender loans. Hence, coefficient estimates on the dummy variables are interpreted as the change in the variance of the residuals relative to sole lender loans. Coefficient estimates for all dummy variables are at least statistically significant at the 10 percent level in column (3), and the coefficients on the dummy variables in the fourth column are statistically significant at the 5 percent level for the third quartile, and statistically significant at the 1 percent level for the fourth quartile. The results in columns (5)-(8) are similar to those in columns (1)-(4). The coefficient on the log of the number of lenders is statistically significant at the 1 percent level and roughly of the same magnitude as the coefficients in columns (1) and (2). In columns (7) and (8), the coefficients are interpreted as the change in residual variance for each quartile relative to the first quartile. In column (7), each coefficient is statistically significant, and in column (8), the coefficients for the third and fourth quartiles are statistically significant. These results suggest that non-price loan terms explain the association between the number of lenders and the residual variance for syndicated loans with below-median numbers of lenders. Overall, the results suggest that the amount of unobservable information impounded in loan spreads is similar for both sole lender loans and syndicated loans with few lenders. Hence, the empirical

17

results suggest that lenders still have incentives to solve asymmetric information problems when the number of lenders in a loan syndicate is not too great.

The results in Table (7) are for specifications where loan ownership is captured by the log of the lead lenders' retained ownership stake in the loan. As in Table (5), results presented in columns (1)-(4) include both sole lender and syndicated loans, and the results in columns (5)-(8) are restricted to syndicated loans. The coefficient on the log of lead banks' ownership stake is positive and statistically different from zero in columns (1), (2), and (5). In addition, the coefficients are smaller when including non-price loan terms in columns (2) and (6). Therefore, our results imply that lead lenders' retained ownership stakes are statistically associated with greater residual variance when including sole lender loans. This is consistent with the assertion that ownership stakes retained by lead lenders provide incentives to solve asymmetric information problems.

The results for quartiles of lead bank ownership in syndicated loans are presented in columns (3), (4), (7), and (8). In column (3) the coefficients for each quartile are statistically different from zero at conventional levels, and the coefficients for the first, second, and third quartiles are only statistically significant in column (4). In addition, in both columns, the coefficients for the first three quartiles are qualitatively similar. In column (7) the coefficients for the third and fourth quartiles are positive and statistically significant, and in column (8) the coefficient for the fourth quartile is positive and statistically significant. Like the results in Table (5), these results suggest that the residual variance does not decrease significantly just because a loan is syndicated; rather, lead lenders must syndicate a substantial portion of the loan. However, the results in column (4) do suggest there is an economically meaningful decline in unobservable information imputed into loan spreads, as the variance of the residuals declines roughly 40 percent for the first through fourth quartiles of lead bank ownership shares. While syndication appears to reduce lead lenders' incentives to gather unobserved information, it does not appear to be the case for all syndicated loans, especially where lead lenders retain large ownership stakes.

The remaining parameter estimates for Tables (3), (5), and (7) are roughly consistent with the assertion that banks gather and incorporate unobservable information in loan spreads for borrowers with observably greater asymmetric information problems. Lead banks incorporate more unobservable information into loan spreads for borrowers with weaker debt ratings, greater leverage, and lower EBITDA. Variables describing banks' financial state do not appear to have much explanatory power for the residual variance. In Table (3), in all but column (5), bank capital has a negative and statistically significant association with the residual variance. This is consistent with the assertion that lenders with a lower likelihood of insolvency or violating capital requirements exert less effort solving asymmetric information, which could potentially be detrimental to lenders' profitability.

The results indicate non-price loan terms influence the amount of unobservable information incorporated into loan spreads. Lead banks incorporate more unobservable information into loan spreads for borrowers with secured loans and loans with general covenants. Loan spreads incorporate less unobservable information into larger loans and loans with performance pricing.

6. Conclusion

In this paper we provide evidence that loan ownership provides incentives for lenders to overcome asymmetric information problems. We identify asymmetric information problems with the prediction of Leland and Pyle (1977) that loan ownership provides incentives for lenders to mitigate asymmetric information problems by allocating resources to acquiring borrowers' private, non-public information regarding their own creditworthiness. We use a heteroskedastic regression to provide evidence of a positive association between several measures of loan ownership by lenders with responsibility for negotiating loan contract terms, and the quantity of non-publicly observable information incorporated into interest rate spreads on corporate loans. However, the amount of unobservable information imputed into loan interest rate spreads is similar for loans provided by a single lender, syndicated loans with fewer lenders, and syndicated loans whose lead lenders retain large ownership stakes. We suggest our results are consistent with the assertion that adverse selection and/or moral hazard problems exist in the corporate loan market, and that ownership stakes provide lenders with the necessary incentives to overcome asymmetric information problems by gathering borrowers' private information regarding their creditworthiness. Our results are important because they suggest that originating loans for distribution or, to put it differently, originating loans without the intention of bearing complete losses in the event of a borrowers' default, weakens but does not completely eliminate lenders' incentives to overcome asymmetric information problems.

References

Akerlof, G. A., 1970. The market for 'lemons': Quality uncertainty and the market mechanism, The Quarterly Journal of Economics 84 (3), 488–500.

Ausubel, L., 1999. Adverse selection in the credit card market, Working paper, Department of Economics, University of Maryland.

Booth, J. R., Booth, L. C., 2006. Loan collateral decisions and corporate borrowing costs, Journal of Money Credit and Banking 38 (1), 67–90.

Boyd, J. H., Prescott, E. C., April 1986. Financial intermediary-coalitions, Journal of Economic Theory 38 (2), 211–232.

Carey, M., Post, M., Sharpe, S. A., 1998. Does corporate lending by banks and financial companies differ: Evidence on specialization in private debt contracting, The Journal of Finance 53 (3).

Chiappori, P.-A., Jullien, B., Salanie, F., 2006. Asymmetric information in insurance: General testable implications, Rand Journal of Economics 37, 783–798.

Chiappori, P.-A., Salanie, F., 2000. Testing for asymmetric information in insurance markets, Journal of Political Economy 108, 57–78.

Degryse, H., Cerqueiro, G., Ongena, S., September 2007. Rules versus discretion in loan rate setting, CESifo Working Paper Series No. 2091.

Dennis, S., Mullineaux, D., 2000. Syndicated loans, Journal of Financial Intermediation 9, 404–426.

Diamond, D., 1984. Financial intermediation and delegated monitoring, Review of Economic Studies 51, 393–414.

Diamond, D., 1991. Monitoring and reputation: The choice between bank loans and directly placed debt, Journal of Political Economy 99, 689–721.

Esty, B., Megginson, W., 2003. Creditor rights, enforcement and debt ownership structure, Journal of Financial and Quantitative Analysis 38, 37–59.

Flannery, M., 1986. Asymmetric information and risky debt maturity choice, The Journal of Finance 41, 18–38.

Gorton, G., Pennacchi, G., 1990. Financial intermediaries and liquidity creation, The Journal of Finance 45 (1), 49–71.

Gorton, G., Pennacchi, G., 1995. Banks and loan sales: Marketing non-marketable assets, The Journal of Finance 35, 389–411.

Grossman, S., Stiglitz, J., 1980. On the impossibility of informationally efficient markets, American Economic Review 70 (3), 393–408.

Holmstrom, B., Tirole, J., 1997. Financial intermediation, loanable funds, and the real sector, Quarterly Journal of Economics 112, 663–691.

Hubbard, R. G., Kuttner, K., Palia, D., 2002. Are there bank effects in borrowers' costs of funds? evidence from a matched sample of borrowers and banks., Journal of Business 75 (4), 559–581.

Iannotta, G., June 2008. Market dicipline in the banking industry: Evidence from spread dispersion, CAREFIN Research Paper 6/08.

Ivashina, V., 2008. Asymmetric information effects on syndicated loan rates, Harvard Business School Working Paper.

Jaffee, D., Russell, T., December 1976. Imperfect information, uncertainty, and credit rationing, The Quarterly Journal of Economics 90 (4), 1074–76.

Jones, J., Lang, W., Nigro, P., 2000. Recent trends in bank loan syndications: Evidence for 1995 to 1999, Office of the Comptroller of the Currency Working Paper.

Lee, S., Mullineaux, D., 2004. Monitoring, financial distress, and the structure of commercial lending syndicates, Financial Management 33 (3).

Leland, H., Pyle, D., 1977. Informational asymmetries, financial structure, and financial intermediation, The Journal of Finance 32 (2), 371–387.

Panyagometh, K., Roberts, G., 2002. Private information, incentive conflicts, and determinants of loan syndications, York University Working Paper 20, 577–593.

Preece, D., Mullineaux, D., 1996. Monitoring, loan renegotiability, and firm value: The role of lending syndicates, Journal of Banking and Finance 20, 577–593.

Qian, J., Strahan, P. E., 2007. How law and institutions shape financial contracts: The case of bank loans, The Journal of Finance 62 (6), 2803–2834.

Rothchild, M., Stiglitz, J., 1976. Equilibrium in competitive insurance markets: An essay on the economics of imperfect information., The Quarterly Journal of Economics 90, 629–649.

Simons, K., 1993. Why do banks syndicate loans?, New England Economic Review, 45–52.

Stiglitz, J., Weiss, A., June 1981. Credit rationing in markets with imperfect information, American Economic Review 71 (3), 393–410.

Strahan, P. E., 1999. Borrower risk and the price and nonprice terms of bank loans, Working Paper.

Sufi, A., 2007. Information asymmetry and financing arrangements: Evidence from syndicated loans, The Journal of Finance 62 (2), 629–668.

Appendix A: Variable Construction

- All-In-Drawn Spread: Taken directly from DEALSCAN database

- Number of Lenders: Log of 1 + number of lenders from DEALSCAN

- Maturity Length: Log of maturity length of loan in days from DEALSCAN

- Deal Amount: Log of deal amount in dollars from DEALSCAN

- Secured/Unsecured Dummy: Equal to 1 if loan is secured, and equal to 0 if loan is unsecured or secured status is missing, from DEALSCAN

- Covenant Dummy: Equal to 1 if loan has either general or financial covenants, from DEALSCAN

- Performance Pricing Dummy: Equal to 1 if loan has performance pricing from DEALSCAN

- Debt Rating: COMPUSTAT item280, takes on increasing values beginning with the most favorable rating and running to least favorable rating

- Research and Development: COMPUSTAT item45/item6

- Leverage: COMPUSTAT (item9 + item34)/item6

- Total Assets: COMPUSTAT log(item6)

- Current Assets: COMPUSTAT item4/data5

- Quick Ratio: COMPUSTAT (item1 + item238 + .6*item2)/item5

- EBITDA: COMPUSTAT (item12+item14)/item6

- Debt Due in One Year: COMPUSTAT item44/(item9 + item34)

- Dividends: COMPUSTAT (item19 + item21)/item6

- Tobin's Average Q: COMPUSTAT (item199*item25 + item9 + item34)/item6

- Cumulative Stock Returns: Cumulative stock returns from previous fiscal year from CRSP; stock return is firms' daily stock return minus CRSP daily value weighted index return

- Cumulative Stock Returns: Standard deviation of daily stock returns from previous fiscal year; stock return is firms' daily stock return minus CRSP daily value weighted index return

- Capital: Total holding company equity/Total holding company assets

- Loan Loss Provisions: Total holding company loan loss provisions/Total holding company assets

- Total Assets: Log of total holding company assets

7. Notes to Tables

- ***, **, * Indicates statistical significance at the 1 percent, 5 percent, and 10 percent levels, respectively.

- All Estimates include year, industry, loan purpose, and loan type dummy variables.

- Summary statistics in Table (1) include all observations which exist for the interest rate spread, asymmetric information, credit risk, non-price loan terms, and lead lender variables.

Table 1: Summary Statistics

Variable	N	Standard Deviation	Mean	25th Pct.	Median	75th Pct.
Ownership Variables and Loan Spread						
All-In-Drawn Spread (Basis Points)	6998	114.32	152.73	62.50	125.00	225.00
Number of Lenders	6058	9.31	9.22	3.00	7.00	12.00
Lead Ownership Share (Percentage)	1958	36.14	38.08	11.33	20.00	57.14
Asymmetric Information Variables						
Number of Previous Deals	6998	3.69	4.20	1.00	3.00	6.00
Total Assets (Millions)	6998	10402.02	4329.04	286.96	991.22	3432.43
Standard Dev. Stock Returns	6998	.07	0.12	0.07	0.10	0.14
Stock Trading Volume	6998	1.17	1.43	0.65	1.11	1.83
Market-to-Book	6998	1.69	1.51	0.58	1.01	1.80
Research and Development Expense	6998	.05	0.02	0.00	0.00	0.02
Credit Risk Variables						
Leverage	6998	0.25	0.34	0.18	0.30	0.43
EBITDA	6998	0.10	0.10	0.07	0.10	0.15
Current Ratio	6998	1.06	1.86	1.17	1.63	2.26
Quick Ratio	6998	0.71	0.80	0.42	0.62	0.95
Debt Due in One Year	6998	0.18	0.10	0.01	0.04	0.12
Debt Rating	6998	5.40	5.20	0.00	5.00	10.00
Non-Price Loan Terms						
Secured/Unsecured	6998	0.49	0.42	0.00	0.00	1.00
Financial Covenants	6998	0.48	0.65	0.00	1.00	1.00
General Covenants	6998	0.49	0.58	0.00	1.00	1.00
Performance Pricing	6998	0.50	0.49	0.00	0.00	1.00
Loan Amount (Millions)	6998	741.67	374.43	50.00	165.00	400.00
Maturity Length (Days)	6755	710.82	1364.62	730.00	1528.00	1826.00
Lead Lender Variables						
Capital	6998	0.01	0.08	0.07	0.08	0.09
Loan Loss Provisions	6998	0.00	0.00	0.00	0.00	0.01
Total Assets (Millions)	6998	562.09	687.90	185.79	632.57	1157.25

Table 2: Results-Mean Equation-Number of Lenders

Variable	(1)	(2)
Asymmetric Information Variables		
Number of Previous Deals	0.40	0.37
	(0.54)	(0.45)
Total Assets	-17.04***	-15.64***
	(1.92)	(1.74)
Std. Dev. Stock Returns	332.02***	311.06***
	(34.57)	(36.66)
Stock Trading Volume	-2.97*	-3.04**
	(1.60)	(1.32)
Market-to-Book	-0.17	-0.57
	(1.17)	(1.03)
Research and Development	118.10**	116.73***
	(47.04)	(42.73)
Credit Risk Variables		
Debt Rating	10.18***	8.91***
	(1.10)	(1.14)
Leverage	50.97***	49.94***
	(7.89)	(7.02)
EBITDA	-198.05***	-168.48***
	(20.11)	(18.33)
Current Ratio	-8.46***	-6.21***
	(2.59)	(2.25)
Quick Ratio	9.09**	7.14*
	(4.30)	(3.78)
Debt Due in One Year	20.37**	12.20
	(9.56)	(8.22)
Lead Lender Variables		
Capital	-196.74	-131.06
	(129.37)	(96.83)
Loan Loss Provisions	1073.27	811.76
	(684.18)	(590.39)
Total Assets	-6.34***	-5.27***
		(21.36)
Constant	341.71***	303.68***
	(36.35)	(32.38)

Table 3: Results-Variance Residuals Equation-Syndicated/Sole Lender

Variable	(1)	(2)
Ownership Variables		
Syndicated	-0.20**	-0.05
	(0.08)	(0.09)
Asymmetric Information Variables		
Number of Previous Deals	-0.00	0.00
	(0.01)	(0.01)
Total Assets	-0.03	0.00
	(0.02)	(0.02)
Std. Dev. Stock Returns	0.42	0.41
	(0.33)	(0.39)
Stock Trading Volume	0.05**	0.04**
	(0.02)	(0.02)
Market-to-Book	-0.02	-0.02*
	(0.01)	(0.01)
Research and Development	0.05	-0.08
	(0.37)	(0.35)
Credit Risk Variables		
Debt Rating	0.08***	0.07***
	(0.01)	(0.01)
Leverage	0.21**	0.26***
	(0.09)	(0.08)
EBITDA	-1.21***	-0.91***
	(0.16)	(0.15)
Current Ratio	-0.06**	-0.03
	(0.03)	(0.03)
Quick Ratio	0.08*	0.06
	(0.04)	(0.04)
Debt Due in One Year	0.16*	0.09
	(0.09)	(0.09)
Lead Lender Variables		
Capital	-3.51**	-4.33***
	(1.56)	(1.44)
Loan Loss Provisions	14.75**	12.80*
	(7.33)	(6.80)
Total Assets	-0.03**	-0.02
	(0.01)	(0.01)
Non-Price Loan Term Variables		
Secured/Unsecured		0.31***
		(0.05)
Financial Covenants		0.07
		(0.06)
General Covenants		0.14**
		(0.05)
Performance Pricing		-0.47***
		(0.04)
Loan Amount		-0.08***
		(0.02)
Loan Maturity Length		-0.02
		(0.02)
Constant	5.64***	6.58***
	(0.37)	(0.43)
N	6982	6739

Table 4: Results-Mean Equation-Number of Lenders

Variable	(1)	(2)	(3)	(4)	(5)	(6)	(7)	(8)
Asymmetric Information Variables								
Number of Previous Deals	0.33	0.39	0.36	0.42	0.20	0.23	0.41	0.45
	(0.55)	(0.46)	(0.55)	(0.46)	(0.53)	(0.44)	(0.55)	(0.46)
Total Assets	-15.45***	-14.63***	-15.96***	-15.11***	-12.92***	-12.29***	-15.56***	-14.73***
	(2.01)	(1.84)	(2.00)	(1.84)	(2.05)	(1.79)	(2.03)	(1.86)
Std. Dev. Stock Returns	329.41***	304.54***	323.36***	300.57***	354.01***	308.28***	329.12***	303.81***
	(35.29)	(35.15)	(34.15)	(34.62)	(38.08)	(37.55)	(34.98)	(35.06)
Stock Trading Volume	-2.94*	-3.17**	-3.10**	-3.27**	-2.93*	-2.97**	-2.94*	-3.16**
	(1.58)	(1.34)	(1.54)	(1.32)	(1.57)	(1.30)	(1.56)	(1.33)
Market-to-Book	0.07	-0.30	-0.01	-0.35	0.49	0.04	0.21	-0.24
	(1.31)	(1.17)	(1.28)	(1.14)	(1.29)	(1.13)	(1.33)	(1.19)
Research and Development	113.31**	113.38**	120.56**	115.01**	64.81	74.68	114.48**	114.73**
	(55.04)	(50.81)	(49.89)	(46.75)	(65.76)	(57.38)	(54.14)	(50.12)
Credit Risk Variables								
Debt Rating	10.96***	9.85***	10.92***	9.91***	11.44***	10.20***	10.99***	9.91***
	(1.23)	(1.25)	(1.22)	(1.24)	(1.30)	(1.34)	(1.25)	(1.27)
Leverage	50.54***	50.51***	51.32***	50.33***	48.41***	46.57***	50.70***	50.12***
	(8.41)	(7.67)	(8.40)	(7.55)	(8.58)	(7.78)	(8.57)	(7.76)
EBITDA	-201.92***	-174.42***	-195.61***	-171.40***	-200.04***	-165.88***	-200.28***	-172.60***
	(21.88)	(19.66)	(21.04)	(18.68)	(25.27)	(22.65)	(22.25)	(19.85)
Current Ratio	-7.74***	-5.96**	-7.92***	-6.40***	-6.25**	-5.03**	-7.61***	-5.99**
	(2.67)	(2.39)	(2.60)	(2.33)	(2.96)	(2.51)	(2.67)	(2.39)
Quick Ratio	10.51**	7.88*	10.36**	8.27**	10.72**	7.45*	10.59**	7.98*
	(4.68)	(4.23)	(4.48)	(4.03)	(5.10)	(4.48)	(4.68)	(4.22)
Debt Due in One Year	18.55*	9.92	20.32**	11.14	10.99	2.06	18.41*	9.95
	(10.42)	(8.97)	(10.26)	(8.88)	(11.15)	(9.13)	(10.44)	(9.02)
Lead Lender Variables								
Capital	-100.47	-54.85	-132.11	-72.90	-127.71	-77.26	-98.44	-48.45
	(124.59)	(98.92)	(128.43)	(100.51)	(128.06)	(93.94)	(124.66)	(98.06)
Loan Loss Provisions	740.14	588.26	1147.42	951.02	1253.28	835.57	805.96	660.72
	(789.09)	(681.93)	(800.39)	(700.03)	(925.03)	(744.12)	(788.05)	(684.00)
Total Assets	-6.22***	-5.69***	-6.61***	-6.12***	-3.33*	-3.10*	-6.13***	-5.69***
	(1.66)	(1.63)	(1.64)	(1.61)	(1.77)	(1.70)	(1.67)	(1.64)
Constant	362.74***	281.53***	347.74***	328.45***	286.91***	209.75***	358.32***	280.96***
	(37.20)	(33.16)	(36.48)	(42.56)	(39.66)	(33.74)	(37.28)	(33.54)

Table 5: Results-Variance Residuals Equation-Number of Lenders

Variable	(1)	(2)	(3)	(4)	(5)	(6)	(7)	(8)
Ownership Variables								
Number of Lenders	-0.15***	-0.09***			-0.15***	-0.08**		
	(0.03)	(0.03)			(0.03)	(0.04)		
First Quartile Number of Lenders			-0.19*	-0.13				
			(0.11)	(0.11)				
Second Quartile Number of Lenders			-0.29***	-0.14			-0.13**	-0.03
			(0.11)	(0.12)			(0.06)	(0.06)
Third Quartile Number of Lenders			-0.39***	-0.25**			-0.23***	-0.14**
			(0.11)	(0.11)			(0.06)	(0.06)
Fourth Quartile Number of Lenders			-0.57***	-0.35***			-0.40***	-0.24***
			(0.11)	(0.12)			(0.06)	(0.07)
Asymmetric Information Variables								
Number of Previous Deals	0.00	0.00	-0.00	0.00	0.00	0.00	0.00	0.00
	(0.01)	(0.01)	(0.01)	(0.01)	(0.01)	(0.01)	(0.01)	(0.01)
Total Assets	0.01	0.02	0.02	0.03	-0.01	0.00	0.01	0.02
	(0.02)	(0.03)	(0.02)	(0.02)	(0.03)	(0.03)	(0.02)	(0.03)
Std. Dev. Stock Returns	0.34	0.23	0.24	0.14	0.39	0.22	0.29	0.20
	(0.35)	(0.36)	(0.34)	(0.35)	(0.40)	(0.39)	(0.35)	(0.36)
Stock Trading Volume	0.05**	0.03*	0.04**	0.03	0.06**	0.04**	0.05**	0.03*
	(0.02)	(0.02)	(0.02)	(0.02)	(0.02)	(0.02)	(0.02)	(0.02)
Market-to-Book	-0.01	-0.01	-0.01	-0.01	-0.01	-0.01	-0.00	-0.01
	(0.01)	(0.01)	(0.01)	(0.01)	(0.02)	(0.01)	(0.01)	(0.01)
Research and Development	-0.04	0.01	0.10	0.14	0.20	0.42	-0.04	-0.00
	(0.43)	(0.41)	(0.38)	(0.37)	(0.62)	(0.61)	(0.44)	(0.41)
Credit Risk Variables								
Debt Rating	0.09***	0.08***	0.09***	0.07***	0.08***	0.07***	0.09***	0.07***
	(0.01)	(0.01)	(0.01)	(0.01)	(0.02)	(0.02)	(0.01)	(0.01)
Leverage	0.22**	0.26***	0.22**	0.24***	0.21**	0.22***	0.23**	0.26***
	(0.10)	(0.09)	(0.10)	(0.09)	(0.09)	(0.08)	(0.10)	(0.09)
EBITDA	-1.25***	-0.85***	-1.16***	-0.77***	-1.80***	-1.43***	-1.24***	-0.84***
	(0.17)	(0.17)	(0.17)	(0.16)	(0.27)	(0.24)	(0.17)	(0.17)
Current Ratio	-0.04	-0.01	-0.04	-0.01	-0.05	-0.02	-0.04	-0.01
	(0.03)	(0.03)	(0.03)	(0.03)	(0.03)	(0.03)	(0.03)	(0.03)
Quick Ratio	0.07	0.03	0.06	0.03	0.06	0.03	0.07	0.03
	(0.05)	(0.04)	(0.04)	(0.04)	(0.05)	(0.05)	(0.05)	(0.04)
Debt Due in One Year	0.20**	0.13	0.19**	0.12	0.29**	0.19*	0.20**	0.14
	(0.10)	(0.09)	(0.10)	(0.09)	(0.12)	(0.11)	(0.10)	(0.09)
Lead Lender Variables								
Capital	-4.10**	-5.16***	-4.24***	-4.82***	-3.14	-3.88**	-4.19***	-5.03***
	(1.61)	(1.53)	(1.60)	(1.50)	(1.97)	(1.79)	(1.60)	(1.51)
Loan Loss Provisions	10.00	11.57	13.62	15.11*	18.07	13.67	9.13	12.15
	(9.19)	(8.54)	(8.59)	(7.97)	(11.21)	(10.48)	(9.14)	(8.46)
Total Assets	-0.01	-0.00	-0.02	-0.01	-0.02	0.00	-0.01	-0.00
	(0.02)	(0.02)	(0.01)	(0.02)	(0.02)	(0.02)	(0.02)	(0.02)
Non-Price Loan Term Variables								
Secured/Unsecured		0.32***		0.31***		0.39***		0.32***
		(0.06)		(0.06)		(0.07)		(0.06)
Financial Covenants		0.08		0.07		0.16**		0.09
		(0.06)		(0.06)		(0.08)		(0.06)
General Covenants		0.16***		0.17***		0.06		0.15***
		(0.06)		(0.06)		(0.08)		(0.06)
Performance Pricing		-0.47***		-0.47***		-0.49***		-0.47***
		(0.04)		(0.04)		(0.05)		(0.04)
Loan Amount		-0.08***		-0.07***		-0.09***		-0.07***
		(0.02)		(0.02)		(0.02)		(0.02)
Loan Maturity Length		-0.00		-0.01		-0.01		-0.00
		(0.03)		(0.02)		(0.03)		(0.03)
Constant	5.45***	6.38***	4.66***	5.85***	5.69***	6.28***	5.30***	6.19***
	(0.39)	(0.50)	(0.34)	(0.46)	(0.43)	(0.51)	(0.38)	(0.50)
N	6227	6002	6227	6002	5827	5618	5827	5618

Table 6: Results-Mean Equation-Lender Share

Variable	(1)	(2)	(3)	(4)	(5)	(6)	(7)	(8)
Asymmetric Information Variables								
Number of Previous Deals	0.00	0.00	-0.00	0.00	0.00	0.00	0.00	0.00
	(0.01)	(0.01)	(0.01)	(0.01)	(0.01)	(0.01)	(0.01)	(0.01)
Total Assets	-16.95***	-15.00***	-16.75***	-14.80***	-11.04***	-9.98***	-11.57***	-10.45***
	(2.41)	(2.08)	(2.41)	(2.11)	(2.69)	(1.87)	(2.80)	(1.87)
Std. Dev. Stock Returns	354.94***	269.04***	363.86***	273.37***	359.96***	210.06***	361.58***	215.16***
	(62.23)	(56.33)	(61.54)	(56.84)	(65.74)	(51.27)	(68.75)	(53.68)
Stock Trading Volume	-1.84	-2.28	-2.05	-2.20	-2.59	-1.41	-2.36	-1.44
	(2.26)	(1.75)	(2.23)	(1.76)	(2.20)	(1.65)	(2.19)	(1.60)
Market-to-Book	-1.76	-2.18*	-1.69	-2.16*	-1.79	-2.22**	-2.05	-2.46**
	(1.49)	(1.17)	(1.41)	(1.14)	(1.33)	(1.09)	(1.48)	(1.11)
Research and Development	42.76	42.55	52.43	41.36	-30.85	13.65	-8.12	36.42
	(60.49)	(38.95)	(57.72)	(37.70)	(58.75)	(33.02)	(66.64)	(32.37)
Credit Risk Variables								
Debt Rating	8.02***	7.49***	8.20***	7.67***	9.08***	7.91***	9.08***	8.15***
	(1.65)	(1.34)	(1.61)	(1.31)	(1.99)	(1.28)	(2.05)	(1.26)
Leverage	30.45***	30.56***	32.80***	31.52***	16.72	20.37**	15.28	21.46**
	(10.99)	(8.94)	(11.17)	(9.13)	(10.68)	(8.47)	(11.26)	(8.67)
EBITDA	-128.50***	-87.69***	-125.92***	-87.04***	-83.66**	-43.49	-87.23**	-48.47*
	(28.77)	(25.79)	(28.55)	(25.92)	(34.35)	(27.54)	(38.14)	(28.38)
Current Ratio	-5.78*	-3.78	-5.62*	-3.68	-2.68	-1.24	-3.89	-1.19
	(3.35)	(2.75)	(3.22)	(2.71)	(3.48)	(2.51)	(3.46)	(2.46)
Quick Ratio	12.17**	7.32	11.58**	6.69	5.95	1.39	7.12	1.32
	(6.09)	(4.80)	(5.85)	(4.61)	(6.54)	(4.12)	(6.96)	(4.15)
Debt Due in One Year	36.25**	16.18	34.86**	16.51	28.41	5.09	29.23	1.41
	(16.57)	(11.74)	(16.25)	(11.30)	(24.13)	(11.14)	(23.27)	(9.63)
Lead Lender Variables								
Capital	-22.86	-3.87	-1.26	5.22	48.32	49.61	48.79	34.65
	(166.28)	(117.49)	(163.78)	(114.85)	(175.26)	(79.91)	(192.72)	(83.33)
Loan Loss Provisions	1823.49*	1419.39*	1903.47*	1450.27*	548.16	723.52	159.77	796.60
	(1007.61)	(758.64)	(1028.67)	(768.85)	(1087.32)	(659.49)	(1120.06)	(708.72)
Total Assets	-5.43**	-5.25***	-5.10**	-5.06**	-1.06	-3.19	-2.01	-3.42*
	(2.38)	(2.00)	(2.55)	(2.09)	(2.97)	(2.11)	(3.62)	(2.08)
Constant	361.03***	311.51***	348.44***	306.34***	329.69***	207.06***	176.16*	251.01***
	(76.53)	(45.14)	(80.57)	(46.29)	(56.96)	(50.34)	(92.84)	(69.41)

Table 7: Results-Variance of Residuals-Lender Share

Variable	(1)	(2)	(3)	(4)	(5)	(6)	(7)	(8)
Ownership Variables								
Lead Ownership Share	0.27***	0.13**			0.23***	0.07		
	(0.05)	(0.06)			(0.07)	(0.06)		
First Quartile Lead Ownership Share			-0.71***	-0.40***				
			(0.14)	(0.15)				
Second Quartile Lead Ownership Share			-0.66***	-0.34**			0.14	0.08
			(0.12)	(0.14)			(0.09)	(0.08)
Third Quartile Lead Ownership Share			-0.66***	-0.41***			0.22**	-0.00
			(0.11)	(0.12)			(0.10)	(0.09)
Fourth Quartile Lead Ownership Share			-0.24**	-0.09			0.61***	0.23**
			(0.11)	(0.11)			(0.13)	(0.10)
Asymmetric Information								
Number of Previous Deals	-0.01	-0.00	-0.01	-0.00	-0.02*	-0.01	-0.00	0.00
	(0.01)	(0.01)	(0.01)	(0.01)	(0.01)	(0.01)	(0.01)	(0.01)
Total Assets	0.02	0.04	0.03	0.04	-0.05	-0.06	-0.04	-0.01
	(0.04)	(0.04)	(0.04)	(0.04)	(0.05)	(0.05)	(0.05)	(0.04)
Std. Dev. Stock Returns	1.89***	1.91***	1.78***	1.90***	2.73***	1.72**	2.06***	1.75***
	(0.63)	(0.60)	(0.61)	(0.59)	(0.79)	(0.68)	(0.75)	(0.64)
Stock Trading Volume	0.06	0.03	0.05	0.02	0.06	0.03	0.05	0.01
	(0.04)	(0.03)	(0.03)	(0.03)	(0.05)	(0.03)	(0.05)	(0.03)
Market-to-Book	-0.05***	-0.05***	-0.04***	-0.05***	-0.05*	-0.03	-0.05	-0.04*
	(0.01)	(0.01)	(0.02)	(0.01)	(0.03)	(0.03)	(0.03)	(0.03)
Research and Development	-0.26	-0.45	-0.31	-0.50	-1.00	-0.89	-0.27	-0.32
	(0.49)	(0.44)	(0.48)	(0.44)	(1.25)	(1.07)	(1.08)	(0.75)
Credit Risk Variables								
Debt Rating	0.08***	0.05***	0.08***	0.05***	0.05	-0.00	0.08**	0.01
	(0.02)	(0.02)	(0.02)	(0.02)	(0.04)	(0.02)	(0.04)	(0.02)
Leverage	0.35**	0.32**	0.33**	0.32**	0.36**	0.39***	0.28*	0.29**
	(0.16)	(0.13)	(0.15)	(0.13)	(0.16)	(0.15)	(0.16)	(0.14)
EBITDA	-0.99***	-0.73***	-0.83***	-0.65***	-2.40***	-1.99***	-2.34***	-1.72***
	(0.29)	(0.24)	(0.29)	(0.23)	(0.56)	(0.40)	(0.55)	(0.40)
Current Ratio	-0.06	0.00	-0.06	-0.01	-0.05	-0.02	-0.11*	-0.02
	(0.05)	(0.04)	(0.05)	(0.04)	(0.06)	(0.05)	(0.06)	(0.05)
Quick Ratio	0.14*	0.06	0.14**	0.07	0.10	0.03	0.14	0.04
	(0.07)	(0.07)	(0.07)	(0.06)	(0.10)	(0.08)	(0.09)	(0.07)
Debt Due in One Year	0.22	0.11	0.21	0.10	0.66**	0.32	0.52*	0.13
	(0.16)	(0.15)	(0.16)	(0.15)	(0.28)	(0.23)	(0.27)	(0.22)
Lead Lender Variables								
Capital	-2.24	-2.71	-1.72	-2.47	-0.45	0.95	-0.33	-0.02
	(2.29)	(2.21)	(2.28)	(2.10)	(3.37)	(2.48)	(3.47)	(2.58)
Loan Loss Provisions	14.10	13.24	16.68	14.87	-1.06	4.03	0.25	13.88
	(10.63)	(10.43)	(10.56)	(10.28)	(17.49)	(15.79)	(17.24)	(15.56)
Total Assets	-0.04*	-0.05**	-0.05**	-0.06**	0.04	-0.02	0.01	-0.03
	(0.02)	(0.02)	(0.02)	(0.02)	(0.05)	(0.04)	(0.05)	(0.04)
Non-Price Loan Term Variables								
Secured/Unsecured		0.60***		0.59***		0.85***		0.79***
		(0.08)		(0.08)		(0.08)		(0.08)
Financial Covenants		-0.03		-0.05		0.01		-0.21
		(0.12)		(0.12)		(0.13)		(0.16)
General Covenants		0.27***		0.27***		0.19*		0.36***
		(0.10)		(0.10)		(0.12)		(0.12)
Performance Pricing		-0.50***		-0.48***		-0.56***		-0.62***
		(0.08)		(0.07)		(0.08)		(0.08)
Loan Amount		-0.09***		-0.08**		-0.09***		-0.13***
		(0.03)		(0.03)		(0.03)		(0.03)
Loan Maturity Length		-0.06*		-0.06*		0.03		0.03
		(0.04)		(0.03)		(0.05)		(0.04)
Constant	4.35***	6.11***	5.60***	6.67***	2.46**	4.43***	4.23***	6.85***
	(0.78)	(0.76)	(0.74)	(0.63)	(1.06)	(1.03)	(1.02)	(0.87)
N	1958	1940	1958	1940	1500	1498	1551	1549

www.ingramcontent.com/pod-product-compliance
Lightning Source LLC
Chambersburg PA
CBHW052027280526
45793CB00005B/1150